# Preface

This book discusses the use of image based neural networks for detecting and locating faces in colour images with complex backgrounds. This book is intended to act as an introduction to the area of face detection and as useful information about the best techniques used to develop a system that can duplicate human vision and how systems in general are implemented at present to find a face in an image. We believe that undergraduate University students seeking to work on a similar project for coursework or perhaps a final year dissertation may find this book useful.

An image based neural network technique along with relevant code is presented in this book to demonstrate the implementation of a face detection algorithm. This face detection algorithm employs a normalisation routine to be used on training and test images and a bootstrapping algorithm to aid in the machine learning process.

This algorithm can detect between 67% and 85% of faces from images of varying size, background and quality with an acceptable number of false detections. The neural network approach is known to be highly sensitive to the grey levels in an image however by subjecting each trained and tested image to the routine introduced here - the system sidestepped the problem. The Yale Face database is an excellent resource for the range of faces, poses and lighting effects on the images. The bootstrapping method used to gain non-face datasets proved very successful as early results were very poor until use was made of the new training data. The speed of the system was quite good when average sized images and searched through a limited amount of levels. Testing larger images involves merely changed a few parameters to miss the first few levels of a larger image. This can become as fast as an average sized image and produce some good quality attempts at classification.

We hope that our introduction to the exciting research area of face detection systems and the discussion of a face detection prototype application will add in some way to each reader's knowledge of face detection and location analysis.

# Acknowledgements

Thanks to Dr. Shannon Li, for the guidance given in the development of my undergraduate project from which the bulk of material in this book is derived. I would like to also thank my family and the staff and students of the Department of Computing and Intelligent Systems who aided me in any way in writing this book.

*- Neil*


I dedicate this book to my wonderful sons Levi and Jack and to my beautiful wife Maxine. I would also like to thank my parents who helped me through college.

*- Kevin*

# Table of Contents

# 1   Introduction

As continual research is being conducted in the area of computer vision, one of the most practical applications under vigorous development is in the construction of a robust real-time face detection system. The goal of this book is to present an insight into the techniques associated with face detection and to present a system which is capable of detecting faces in real-time. Successfully constructing a real-time face detection system not only implies a system capable of analyzing video streams, but also naturally leads onto the solution to the problems of extremely constraint testing environments. Analyzing a video sequence is the current challenge since the faces are constantly in dynamic motion, presenting many different possible rotational and illumination conditions. While solutions to the task of face detection are presented, detection performances of many systems are heavily dependent upon a strictly constrained environment. The problem of detecting faces under gross variations remains largely uncovered.

This book addresses the issue of developing a real-time face detection system. The design of this system is based upon a Neural Network approach. This system builds on previously used techniques and we use these to further develop a novel face detection system. We hope that the system presented here can be further used to build reliable face detection systems. The algorithm presented here can detect between 67% and 85% of faces from images of varying size, background and quality with an acceptable number of false detections. It can detect between 'face' and 'non-face'. One of the most important components of the system is the normalisation routine. This is a technique that makes training data and test data uniform and where lighting is involved it can drastically affect the classifying of images.

The next section presents a background overview of the area of face detection. Further chapters present the neural network face detection prototype and explain the usage, implementation and findings of using such a basic face detection system.

# 2    Face Detection

The face is the most distinctive and widely used key to a person's identity. The area of face detection has attracted considerable attention in the advancement of human-machine interaction as it provides a natural and efficient way to communicate between humans and machines. The problem of detecting the faces and facial parts in image sequences has become a popular area of research due to emerging applications in intelligent human-computer interface, surveillance systems, content-based image retrieval, video conferencing, financial transaction, forensic applications, pedestrian detection, image database management system and so on. Face detection is essentially localising and extracting a face region from the background. This may seem like an easy task but the human face is a dynamic object and has a high degree of variability in its appearance, which makes face detection a difficult problem in computer vision.

Consider the pictures in Fig 2.1 these are typical images that could be used in face classification research. They have no background and are all front facing. Any face detection program should have no trouble in detecting these. However Fig 2.2 shows a realistic application scenario. It has a complex background with face like colours and the face size is very small in proportion to the image.

**Fig 2.1:** Images that could be used for face classification

A wide variety techniques have been developed ranging from simple edge-based algorithms to composite high level approaches using advanced pattern recognition methods [2,3,4,7,14].

**Fig 2.2:** A realistic face detection scenario

Face detection can be established by two approaches: (i) a feature-based method and (ii) an image-based method.

## 2.1 Feature Based Method to Face Detection

This area contains techniques that are classified as low-level analysis. These are methods that that deal with the segmentation of visual features using pixel properties such as gray-scale and colour. The features that these low-level methods detect can be ambiguous, but these methods are easy to implement and fast. (*See: Edges, Colour segmentation*) Another area of techniques called feature analysis, where face detection is based upon facial features using information of face geometry. Through feature analysis, feature ambiguities are reduced and locations of the face and facial features are determined. (*See: Feature searching*). The last group involves the use of active shape models. These have been developed for the purpose of complex and non-rigid feature extraction such as eyes and lip tracking. (*See: Snakes and Point Distributed Models*)

## Low-level Analysis

*Edges:* This is the most primitive feature in face detection applications. The earliest of this work was done by Sakai *et al* [1]. Most of the work was based on basic line drawings of faces from photographs, aiming to locate facial features. Further work was carried out by Craw *et al* [7] whose work led to tracing a human head outline. This was the basis of the detection program, where the next step was feature analysis to determine if the shape detected was indeed a human face shape. Edge detection essentially locates major outlines in the image (the threshold can be set to detect predominant lines or indeed all lines). It then assigns each pixel on the line with a binary digit to set it out from the back ground. Many types of edge operators exist, they all operate on the same premise and give similar results. The examples (Figs 2.3 – 2.6) show some of the edge routines applied.

**Fig 2.3:** Original Image

**Fig 2.4:** Sobel edge filtering

**Fig 2.5**: Prewitt edge filtering     **Fig 2.6**: Canny edge filtering

In an edge-detection based approach to face-detection, the edges (after identification) need to be labelled and matched to a face model in order to verify correct detections. Features have to be located and identified such as eyes, hairline or jaw line. If these all seem to be in ratio and in place a face is detected.

This method is accurate in images with no complex backgrounds and the face needs to be in clear view facing front. These limitations sometimes restrict edge detection implemented as a pre-processing tool to identify face shapes and then these figures are handed over to a pattern based system for more accurate detection process.

*Colour Segmentation:*     The detection of skin colour in colour images is a very popular and useful technique for face detection. This section explains an approach for determining the skin coloured parts of an image. Many Techniques have reported locating skin colour regions in an image[2,3,5,16]. While the input colour image is typically in the RGB format, the RGB model is not used in the detection process. It is well known that the RGB colour model is not a reliable model for detecting skin colour. This is because RGB components are subject to luminance change, this means face detection may fail if the lighting condition changes from image to image.

The technique usually uses colour components in the colour space, such as HSV or YCbCr [3]. The colour model used here is the YIQ model, a universal colour space used for colour television transmission. The conversion of RGB to YIQ components is done by using the formula (1):

$$\begin{bmatrix} Y \\ I \\ Q \end{bmatrix} = \begin{bmatrix} 0.299 & 0.587 & 0.114 \\ 0.596 & -0.275 & -0.320 \\ 0.212 & -0.523 & 0.311 \end{bmatrix} \begin{bmatrix} R \\ G \\ B \end{bmatrix} \qquad (1)$$

Where R,G,B are the red, green and blue component values which exist in the range [0,255]. The YIQ colour model a colour is described by three attributes: luminance, hue and saturation.[2] Y represents the luminance channel while I and Q represent the two chrominance channels, hue and saturation. It has been found that the I and Q components for skin colour fall within a narrow band (2). Human skin colour lies in a tight cluster in colour spaces even when faces of different races are considered. This band sets the threshold for YIQ skin colour segmentation.

$$(60 < Y < 200) \text{ AND } (20 < I < 50) \qquad (2)$$

This threshold can be changed throughout the running of a system. The YIQ conversion also effectively suppresses the background of other colours and allows the detection of small faces in a natural environment.

## Feature Analysis

*Feature Searching:* Feature searching works on the premise that it exclusively looks for prominent facial features in the image. After this main detection less prominent features are searched for using standard measurements of facial geometry. A pair of eyes is the most commonly applied reference feature [12, 13, 16]. Other features include the top of the head and the main face axis. This method is often combined with edge detection where the edge densities are detected from a top-down approach starting from the top of the head. These are measured and after distinguishing a reference measurement. These measurements are plotted against the average lengths of facial measurements (which is found by measuring a set of varying face images held on a database). Fig 2.7 shows a table showing the average measurements in respect to reference length obtained from the modelling of 42 frontal faces in a database.

**Average Lengths (Times the Reference Length) of Facial Features**

|  | Head height | Eye Separation | Eye to Nose | Eye to Mouth |
|---|---|---|---|---|
| Average Length | 1.972 | 0.516 | 0.303 | 0.556 |

**Fig 2.7:** De Silva's *et al*[19] findings.

This method does not rely on skin colour and so manages to detect various races. This method is also restricted to frontal face images with a plain background and it need a clear forehead not hidden by hair to ensure detection. If facial hair, earrings and eyewear are worn on the face it fails to detect the face.

## Active Shape Models

*Snakes:* Snakes (or Active Contours) were first introduced by Kass *et al* [20]. They are commonly used to locate a head boundary. This is done by firstly initialising the snake at the proximity around the head boundary.. The snake locks onto the nearby edges and subsequently assumes the shape of the head. The snakes path is determined by minimising an energy function, $E_{snake}$, denoted as:

$$E_{snake} = E_{internal} + E_{external} , \qquad (3)$$

Where $E_{internal}$, $E_{external}$ are the internal and external energy functions. The internal energy defines the snake's natural evolution and external counteracts the internal energy to enable the contours to deviate from the natural evolution and assume the shape of nearby features – ideally the head boundary. The appropriate energy terms have to be considered. Elastic energy is used commonly as internal energy – this can give the snake the elastic-band characteristic that causes the snake's evolution (by shrinking and expanding). The external energy requirement can include a skin colour function which attracts the skin colour function to the face region. Snakes are well equipped to detect feature boundaries but it still has its problems. The contours often get trapped on false image features causing the program to crash. Snakes also try to keep to the minimum curvature and this can lead to problems as some face shapes may not be completely convex and thus will return false results.

*Point Distributed Models:* This method takes the statistical information of the shape given in an image and compares it to a pre-defined training set to determine whether the shape is a head (or indeed a head shape).[21] The point distributed model created by the program is put into a set of points which are labelled. Variations of these points are first determined by using the training set that includes objects of different sizes and poses. Using principal component analysis, variations of the features in a training set are constructed as a linear flexible model. The model comprises the mean of all the features in the sets and the principle modes of variation for each point where $x$ represents a point on the point distributed model, x is the mean feature in the training set for that point, $P = [p1\ p2\ ...\ pt\ ]$ is the matrix of the $t$ most significant variation vectors of the covariance of deviations, and $v$ is the weight vector for each mode.

$$x = x + Pv \qquad\qquad — \qquad\qquad (4)$$

Face point distribution models were first developed by Lanitis *et al.* as a flexible model. This model defines a global model for a face which includes facial features such as eye-brows, the nose and eyes. Using 152 manually planted control points (x) and 160 training face images, the face point distribution model is obtained. For comparison the mean shape model x is placed on top (or near) the area being tested. The labels of each image are then compared. During the comparison the corresponding points are only allowed to differ in a way that is consistent with the training set data. The global characteristic of the model means that all features can be detected simultaneously so this means that the need for feature searching is removed, cutting down pre-processing time. Another advantage of this technique is that it can detect a face even if a feature is missing – hidden or removed. This is because other feature comparisons can still detect the face. This technique needs to be further developed to detect multiple faces in images.

## Face Detection using Colour Segmentation

A combination of techniques can be used to identify a face. This can increase accuracy. Skin colour segmentation can be used to firstly detect a possible face region in an image and then put this region through a more complex pattern recognition program to identify a face. An image can be tested in the YIQ space to test each pixel to determine and to classify if it's either skin or non-skin [2]. A lookup table is employed to classify the "skinness" of each pixel, where each colour is tested to see if it lies in the range of skin colour and be associated a binary value of one if it is and zero if not. A bounded box is needed to determine the range and location of the values of ones. The purpose of the colour segmentation is to reduce the search space of the subsequent techniques, so it is important to determine as tight a box as possible without cutting off the face.

After the colour image has been mapped into a binary image of ones and zeros representing skin and non-skin regions. It is common during the colour segmentation to return values that are closely skin but non-skin, or other skin-like coloured regions that is not part of the face or the body. These noisy erroneous values are generally isolated pixels or group of pixels that are dramatically smaller than the total face regions. Inclusion of these noisy pixels would result in a box that is much larger than intended and defeat the purpose of the segmentation.

Further morphological refinements are applied to the binary output in order to reduce some of the effects of these noisy pixels. Since these spurious errors are generally much smaller than the face region itself, morphological techniques such as erosion, filtering and closing are good tools to use to eliminate these pixels. These are available in the excellent MATLAB [1] image processing toolbox.

## 2.2 Image Based Approach to Face Detection

The image based approach to face detection is plagued by the unpredictability of image environmental conditions and unpredictable face appearances. The image based approach is usually limited to detecting one face in a non complex background with ideal conditions. They are usually a part of a combined approach. There is a need for techniques that can detect multiple faces with complex backgrounds. The pattern recognition area of face detection was developed for these reasons. This technique works on the idea that the face is recognised by comparing an image to examples of face patterns. This eliminates the use of face knowledge as the detection technique. This means inaccurate or uncompleted data from facial images can still be detected as a face. The approach here is to classify an area as either face or non-face, so a set of face and non-face prototypes must be trained to fit these patterns. These form a 2D intensity array (thus the name image based) to be compared with a 2D array taken from the input image test area. This then decides whether the face falls into a face or non-face type. In the following sections we will present some of the complex techniques that use a feature based approach. These are *Eigenfaces, Neural Networks* and *Support Vector Machines*.

### Eigenfaces

In the late 1980s, Sirovich and Kirby [22] developed a technique using principal component analysis to efficiently represent human faces. Given an ensemble of different face images, the technique first finds the principal components of the distribution of faces, expressed in terms of eigenvectors (taken from a 2D image matrix). Each individual face in the face set can then be approximated by a

---

[1] http://www.mathworks.com/

linear combination of the largest eigenvectors, more commonly referred to as eigenfaces, using appropriate weights. The eigenfaces are determined by performing a principal component analysis on a set of example images with central faces of the same size. In addition the existence of a face in a given image can be determined. By moving a window covering a sub image over the entire image faces can be located within the entire image.

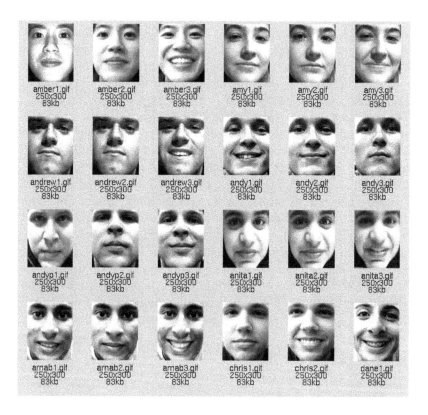

**Fig 2.8:** Images that could be used to comprise a training set

Fig 2.8 shows photographs that could comprise a training set, and it is this training set that the eigenfaces are extracted from. The photographs in the training set are mapped to another set which are the eigenfaces. As with any other mapping in mathematics, we can now think of the data (the photographs and the eigenfaces) as existing in two domains. The photographs in the training set are one of these domains, and the eigenfaces comprise the second domain that is often referred to as the *face space*. Fig 2.9 shows an example of eigenfaces that could be generated to make up the face space.

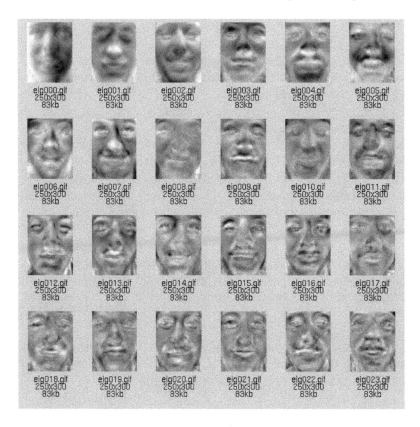

**Fig 2.9:** Possible eigenface images

Now take the eigenfaces that comprise the face space and add them together with appropriate weights to re-compose one of the photographs in the training set. It is through the analysis of these weights that face detection can be realised. A training set of 100 to 150 images should be enough to generate appropriate eigenfaces.

## Neural networks

Neural Networks have become a popular technique for pattern recognition face detection[15,17,18]. They contain a stage made up of multilayer perceptrons. Other techniques are also applied to add to the complexity of its process. Modular architectures, committee–ensemble classification, complex learning algorithms, auto associative and compression networks, and networks evolved or pruned with genetic algorithms are all examples of the widespread use of neural networks in pattern recognition. The first neural approaches were based on Multi-layer perceptrons which gave promising results with fairly simple datasets. The first advanced neural approach which reported results on a large, difficult dataset was by Rowley *et al.* [18]. Their system incorporates face knowledge in a retinally connected neural network shown in Fig. 2.10. The neural network is designed to look at windows of 20 x 20 pixels (thus 400 input units). There is one hidden layer with 26 units, where 4 units look at 10 x 10 pixel subregions, 16 look at 5 x 5 subregions, and 6 look at 20 x 5 pixels overlapping horizontal stripes. The input window is pre-processed through lighting correction (a best fit linear function is subtracted) and histogram equalization. A problem that arises with window scanning techniques is overlapping detections. Rowley *et al.* deals with this problem through two heuristics:

1. Thresholding: the number of detections in a small region surrounding the current location is counted, and if it is above a certain threshold, a face is present at this location.

2. Overlap elimination: when a region is classified as a face according to thresholding, then overlapping detections are likely to be false positives and thus are rejected.

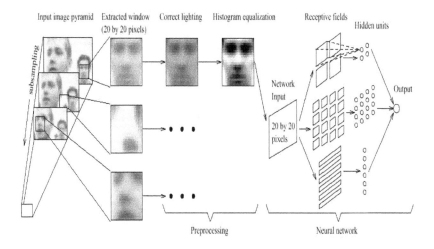

**Fig 2.10:** The system of Rowley *et al.*

During training, the target for a face-image is the reconstruction of the image itself, while for nonface examples, the target is set to the mean of the *n* nearest neighbours of face images. Feraud *et al* [23] employ a training algorithm based on the bootstrap algorithm of Sung and Poggio [5] (and also a similar pre-processing method consisting of histogram equalization and smoothing).

The system is trained with a simple learning rule which promotes and demotes weights in cases of misclassification. Similar to the Eigenface method, Roth *et al*.[24] use the bootstrap method of Sung and Poggio for generating training samples and pre-process all images with histogram equalization. The training set outlined in Fig 2.8 can also be used in this training circumstance.

## Support Vector Machines

Support vector machine is a patter classification algorithm developed by V. Vapnik and his team at AT&T Bell Labs [26,27]. While most machine learning based classification techniques are based on the idea of minimising the error in training data (*empirical risk*) SVM's operate on another induction principle, called *structural risk minimization*, which minimizes an upper bound on the generalization error. Training is performed with a boot-strap learning algorithm.[10] Generating a training set for the SVM is a challenging task because of the difficulty in placing "characteristic" non-face images in a the training set. To get a representative sample of face images is not much of a problem; however, to choose the right combination of non-face images from the immensely large set of such images, is a complicated task.

For this purpose, after each training session, non-faces incorrectly detected as faces are placed in the training set for the next session. This "bootstrap" method overcomes the problem of using a huge set of non-face images in the training set, many of which may not influence the training [5]. To test the image for faces, possible face regions detected by another technique (say, colour segmentation) will only be tested to avoid exhaustive scanning. The testing then begins. In order to explain SVM process consider data points of the form $\{(x_i, y_i)\}\, i=1..N$ , and we wish to determine among the infinite such points in an N-dimensional space which of two classes of such points does a given point belong to. If the two classes are linearly separable, we need to determine a hyper-plane that separates these two classes in space. However, if the classes are not clearly separable, then our objective would be to minimize the smallest generalization error. Intuitively, a good choice is the hyper-plane that leaves the maximum margin between the two classes (margin being defined as the sum of the distances of the hyper-plane from the closest points of the two classes), and minimizes the misclassification errors.

The same data used to train a neural network can be trained here. The learning time for SVM algorithms are significantly smaller than that for the neural network. Back propagation of a neural network takes more time than the required training time of a SVM training period.

## 2.3 Face Detection using Neural Networks

Along with our choice of using skin colour segmentation to test an image for the presence of a face we intend to using Neural networks as the next stage in the detection process. The Colour segmentation will give the result of an area where there is a possibility there is a face. There may be more than one region in the image- be it a face or a face coloured region. This region will be tested using the pattern recognition technique. Testing only the regions brought forward by the colour segmentation stage will cut down processing time and increase accuracy. Of course this accuracy also dependant on how good the program is and how good the training set is. Training sets can be acquired from privately owned or commercial databases or even from locally stored face images.

# 3 Building Face Detection Systems

In order to design a face detection system, it is necessary first to understand what it is that the system should be doing. The process of understanding the task to be undertaken by a neural network face detection system is provided here. This will show the major task broken down into its component parts as illustrated in Fig 3.1. The purpose of the program is to simulate human vision and detect a face from an image, essentially determining which part of an image contains a face. The program aim is to:

1. Accept an image from the user
2. Run the image through a set of processes to detect the presence of a face through:
   (i)    Skin Colour Segmentation; and
   (ii)   Pattern Recognition using Neural Networks.
3. Localise and map the face area
4. Output a final image showing location of face on the image

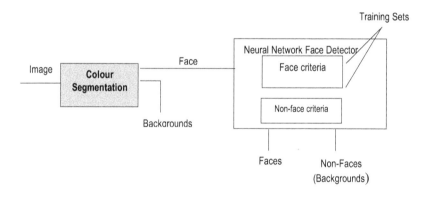

**Fig 3.1:** Requirements of a generic face detection system

The system is composed of two main modules. This does not include the interface. The function of the two main modules are:

## (i)    Colour Segmentation

- Accept an image from the program interface
- Convert this image into the from RGB to YIQ format
- Test the image for the presence of skin coloured pixels
- Create a image of the original showing skin and non-skin pixels
- Clean up image to eradicate early false detections
- Detect and locate potential face areas
- Output areas of image for Neural Network Testing

The colour segmentation stage ensures that no exhaustive unnecessary testing of Neural Network processing. If this was to take place the program would definitely not be close to run-time standard as it takes longer for this program to run. Only select areas of the image that are suspected faces are tested.

## (ii)   Neural Network Based Detection

- A set of images (face and non-face) to be the basis of detection.
- Normalise images to ensure uniform datasets
- Train set of normalised images (face and non-face)
- Accept regions of images from colour segmentation to be tested
- Test the regions of the images
- Determine if region is face or non face
- Find centre of face and mark for output presentation
- Output image with detected face.

A good training set of images needs to be built up (Fig 2.8) that will give acceptable and reliable results. This includes entering non-face images that will classify some obvious non-face detections.

# 4    A Neural Network Detection System

A generic face detection system has 3 major tasks to perform. These are:

1.  Data preparation
2.  Training
3.  Image Scanning and Detection

Each of these tasks is further broken down into separate stages to form the different modules to be programmed. The system presented here adopts two approaches to face detection. The goal being a robust, fast, accurate system that used a combination of techniques. The Skin Colour Segmentation approach reduces the search area a more advanced and time consuming neural network method to search. Fig 4.1 shows a block diagram of the Neural Network face detection system. It shows that the data preparation stage takes place first.

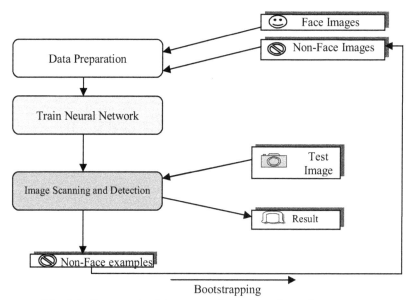

**Fig 4.1:** System Architecture of the face detection system.

The completion of this stage is essential for the next stage to begin. This prepares the training data for the Neural Network training stage. Provisional data is used for the non-face data entered at the first stage, further on in the development of the system a bootstrapping technique is employed to gain non-face data and continually increase accuracy. Once these first two stages are complete and a sufficient data set is built up the face detector can run stand-alone. The successfulness of the face detector is dependant upon the accuracies of the data preparation and training stages. The system is developed using Matlab due to its image processing and neural network toolboxes.

## 4.1   Data Preparation

Inputs to the program need to be in a uniform format in order for the network to obtain accurate results. This area describes how datasets are used to train the network and the manner in which they are prepared for input to the system. This covers resizing, masking and normalising the face and non-face data. In order to train a neural network for face detection we need to input data that can train the network. This input data takes three forms: *Face Data*, *Non-face Data* and a *Face Mask*. These are essential for the system to run accurately and the better the data entered the better the neural net will be. Datasets were gained in different ways.

The face mask is input through a function called *buildmask*. This creates a mask that cuts off surrounding edges of the image rectangle to give an oval shape to the face image. This mask is used to apply to training images (face and non-face) and to use in the rectangle for scanning and testing an image. This is done as all faces are oval in shape. This helps eliminate any false detection as a piece of scenery that appears to the program as a face might not have an oval shape and therefore be eliminated. It also helps in removing any piece of the background image that obstructs the image making it look like a non-face. It confirms that inside the oval is a face. A representation of the mask is shown in Fig 4.2.

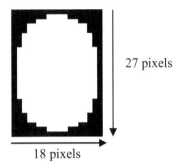

27 pixels

18 pixels

**Fig 4.2:** Face Mask

The size of the rectangle where this mask is contained is 18 x 27 pixels. With the mask applied to an image (training or tested) this gives approximately 400 pixels. The system can scan over the image and pick out rectangles that contain information that tells it that it scan is a face. Rowley et al [18] suggests 400 input units for the training and testing of a network.

An algorithm for the data preparation stage of a neural network face detection system could be as follows:

Load Training data
START
- Build a 18x27 oval image mask
- Edit face image into 18 x 27 pixel rectangle
- Load face training 18x27 pixel images
  - Flip image left and right to expand dataset
  - Normalise Datasets (use Normalise Algorithm)
  - Mask each image with oval image mask within the 18x27 rectangle
  - Create image vectors suitable to use for training
  - Load non-face training images (after manually editing the face image into a 18x27 pixel rectangle). *Note:* that these images are taken from early images using a bootstrapping technique.
  - Flip image left, right and upside-down to expand dataset
  - Normalise Datasets (use Normalise Algorithm)
  - Mask each image with oval image mask within the 18x27 rectangle
  - Create image vectors suitable to use for training

- Aggregate data into labelled data sets and pass the vectors to the training algorithm

END

A face dataset is quite easy to acquire. For instance, we used one courtesy of the Yale face database [14]. We selected 120 face images with a variety of emotions, poses and lighting effects. One can also flip each image left to right to give another version of each face. This database is excellent for the range of faces required for testing and indeed training the network. Examples from the face database are shown in Fig 4.3.

**Fig 4.3:** Examples from the Yale face database

Each face can then be manually edited so that it is 18x27 pixels wide since the faces gained from the database are not already in this usable format. A few examples of the manually edited images are shown in Fig 4.4. These are un-normalised, unmasked images. This is their raw form before they are entered into the data preparation stage.

**Fig 4.4** Examples of training images

Training a neural network for face detection is challenging because of the difficulty in characterising non-face images. Unlike face recognition where the classes to be discriminated are different faces, the two classes to be tested are 'images containing faces' and 'images not containing faces'. It is a simple task to get a representation of faces, but it is a much harder task to get a valid representative of images that do not. Images such as the ones in Fig 4.5 can be passed through the system to represent no-faces.

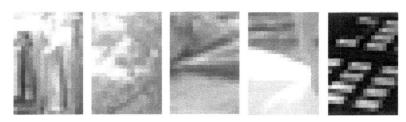

**Fig 4.5:** Random non-face images

These are a random set of images that do not contain face data. These should allow the network to train these and classify them as non-faces. These should be sufficient for the early stage of setting up the network and to give provisional results. Images can also be flipped left to right and upside down to expand the dataset selected. These images can be fed into a neural network and then the network retrained to include these false detections as non-faces. Random images such as the ones in Fig 4.5 can be used initially to set up the network and gain early results. These images may sometimes not have any effect on the classifier as they may not be mistaken for a face. The images intended to be used for bootstrapping should not be redundant so therefore the training set size should only be required to be of essential size. An algorithm for the bootstrapping method could be as follows:

Bootstrapping
START
- Create set of non-face images with images of random pixels
- *Train Neural Network
- Run on scenes that do not contain faces and extract false detections
- Enter these as non-face variables to existing data set.
- Rerun from * to improve the accuracy of system.
END

## Normalisation

The subject of lighting conditions on an image can determine whether or not the face can be classified as an image, or indeed a piece of scenery be mistaken for a face. Neural nets are susceptible to pixel magnitude values. Fig 4.6 shows an image with heavy left and right lighting effects. The system should be able to correct an image with these lighting effects to the point were it is similar to testing the image with no lighting effects (also shown). Sung and Poggio [5] to apply a system of subtracting gradient correlation and then equalising the histogram afterwards to eliminate any lighting effects that may effect the image.

**Fig 4.6:** Image with heavy lighting effects

To apply a similar approach to above, one needs to fit a single linear plane to each image. This plane can be computed efficiently through simple linear projection solving the equation (5) (where X, Y, and Z are the vectors corresponding to their respective coordinate values, 1 is a vector of 1's to compute the constant offset, and C is a vector of three numbers defining the linear slopes in the X and Y directions and the constant offset). To compute C, we simply need to compute equation (6). These coefficients can be used to construct a shading plane that can be subtracted out of the original image.

$$[X \ Y \ 1] * C = Z \qquad (5)$$

$$([X\ Y\ O]\ '\ *\ [X\ Y\ O])\text{^}-1\ *\ [X\ Y\ O]\ '\ *\ Z \tag{6}$$

Once the lighting direction is corrected for, the grayscale histogram can then be rescaled to span the minimum and maximum grayscale levels allowed by the representation. This returns the image as a clean image with no illumination effects. This should be applied to all face and non-face training images and scanned portions of the image in order for 'fair' detection. The algorithm for a normalisation routine follows:

> Normalise Image
> START
> • Input an image
> • Set up a set of shading matrices to subtract from images
> • Shade out an approximation of the shading plane to correct for single light source effects
> • Rescale histogram co that every image has the same gray level range
> • Return Normalised image
> END

## 4.2    Neural Network Training

This stage is the most important stage of the face detection program where a multi-layer perceptron network to identify scanned window patterns as faces or non-faces from their vector of distance measurements needs to be trained.    When trained, the multi-layer perceptron network should receive an input vector of distance measurements.    It takes these and compares it with the trained network data.    It will output a '0.9' for detected face or '-0.9' otherwise. A neural network can be created and trained with the help of MATLAB's Neural Network Toolbox.

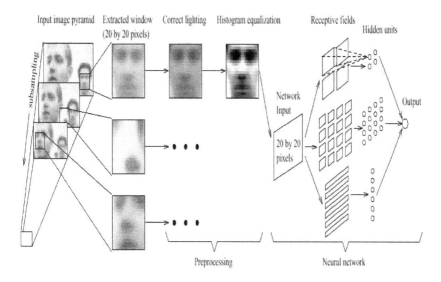

**Fig 4.7:**  Diagram of a Face Detection System [18]

Given the mask size of 18x27 pixels minus the masked region of a image, the number of inputs to the neural network will be approximately 400.    Each of these inputs is connected directly to a corresponding pixel in the image mask.    Good training info passed from data preparation will ensure that training here will classify a face within these 400 pixels. There is 1 output unit of that will either hold the value '0.9' for a successful detection of a face and '-0.9' for scenery. This result is achieved after the scanning stage of the system where every region of the scanned image will be given one of the appropriate values suggesting the presence or absence of a face.

There are 25 hidden units in the network. These hidden units consist of three type of hidden units: 4 which look at 100 pixel sub-regions, 16 which look at 25 pixel sub-regions, and 5 which look at overlapping 20x5 pixel horizontal stripes of pixels. Rowley et al [18 ] suggested that these three types are to be used. These hidden units should allow the network to detect local features that might be important for face detection. In particular, the horizontal stripes allow the hidden units to detect such features such as mouths or pairs of eyes. The square featured receptive fields will detect such areas as single eyes, noses, or corners of a mouth. Fig 4.7 shows a diagram (courtesy of Rowley et al [18]) that can represent a neural network.

## 4.3   Training

A gradient decent error back-propagation is performed to train the neural network for all of the training data. The principle of a feed-forward neural network is to model multi-dimensional linear dependencies in a compact, concise framework. An input vector is presented as input to the network. An output vector of a fixed size is calculated by summing the contributions of all the input values multiplied by their corresponding weights. This process is repeated over all the layers of the neural network, feeding the output of the upstream layer to the input of the downstream layer. Every layer consists of a matrix of weight values. Back-propagation relies on the delta-rule learning equation (7) for neural nets. Essentially, the delta learning rule corrects a neural network's weights so the next time it is presented with a particular example (for which the correct classification is known), its output will be closer to that known correct output, which is also presented with the example. It accomplishes this by crossing the target output vector with the input vector to obtain a matrix that would correctly calculate the target output from the input. It then adds these resulting 'delta' weights into the network's weight matrix.

$$\text{Deltaw\_ji}(n) == \text{eta} * \text{delta\_j} * x\_ji + \text{alpha} * \text{Deltaw\_ji}(n-1) \qquad (7)$$

In a multi-layer network case where we are dealing with hidden layers, delta rule is not as straightforward. In particular, it is difficult to determine what the values of the hidden nodes should be to produce a desired output. In fact, they could be any number of values and the network could still feasibly learn the pattern. This is the nature of the neural network's learning ability, to abstract hidden details of input patterns into hidden nodes. These details are often not perceivable by humans, but they are nonetheless effective means of learning how to classify inputs. For any given set of input-output pairs, the neural net can learn the aspects of a positive set that distinguish it from the negative set by adjusting its weights according to error gradient - and can do so with an entirely different set of hidden weights every time. Back-propagation comes into play when we want to update the weight matrices of the network. In order to determine a reasonable expected value for the hidden layer vector, we take the target output vector and reverse-propagate its values through the weight matrices of the network. Through this process the hidden layers gradually pick up characteristic details that should allow them to differentiate between vector that represent a face and those that represent scenery.

The algorithm for Training the neural network follows:

Train Neural Net
START
• Create Neural Network with 400 input units, 25 hidden units and 1 output unit
• While epochs <500 or there is a decrease in performance on the validation set, perform gradient descent error back propagation:

Input images
For each <x, t> in training examples do:
  • input instance x to the network and compute the output o of every unit u in the network
  • for each network output unit k, calculate its error term delta_k
  • delta_k <- o_k(i - o_k)(t_k - o_k)
  • for each hidden unit h, calculate its error term delta_h
  • delta_h <- o_h(1 - o_h) *  Sigma(k<outputs) w_kh * delta_k
  • update each network weight w_ji
  • w_ji <- w_ji + Deltaw_ji
  • Deltaw_ji = eta * delta_j * x_ji

• Pass created network to scanning routine.
END

## 4.4   Image Scanning and Detection

This is the stage where a test image is introduced and tested by the network. After the image is scanned through and it sub-regions are passed to the network for testing; the program returns a result containing boxed off faces indicating successful detection over the original image.

When an image is entered to be tested, the idea is that the computer will detect the presence of the face (if any) and locate its position on the image. The image can be of any size and in this area the face could be any where – the program is not told where to look. It has to scan every possible area of the image for the presence of a face. A window 27x16 pixels in size (same size as image mask) scan each possible region of the image overlapping each other. Each region is taken out and is first masked with the mask shown in Fig 4.2. This region is then normalised to remove any heavy lighting effects from the image. If the region is a face then its vector parameters should resemble the parameters of the vectors detailed on the network, if this is the case a face is detected. This procedure is illustrated in Fig 4.8. (A) shows the test image and the 18x27 window being scanned repetitively over it. (B) shows what happens to each sub-region that is scanned.

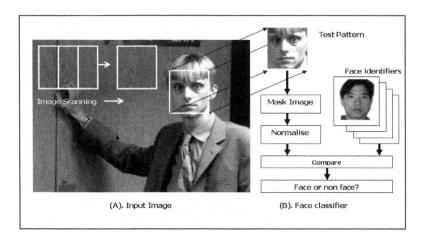

**Fig 4.8:** The Image scanning procedure.

33

When detecting a face in an image the likelihood that every face in every image is contained in a 18x27 pixel window is unlikely. To detect faces that are larger than the window size the image can be repeatedly reduced in size and the image scanned at each size. The image can be scaled down by about 1.2-1.3 each time, this scale factor is suggested by Sung and Poggio [5]. These set of images will be referred to as the image pyramid. If an image of 200*200 pixels is scaled in size; six times the resolution in each should be able to cover all possibilities of faces in the image. The start level of this pyramid can be set to test larger images which do not contain 18*27 pixel sized faces in the images original state. This can cut down unnecessary, exhaustive scanning routines. The number of pyramid levels can also be changed as this can be used in turn with the start level of the pyramid to use the face detector more efficiently on larger images.

To vary how strict the detector is in classifying images, a threshold value can be set to tell the classifier to only return a 0.9 (positive detection) if the section scanned adheres to the parameters of trained data in the network. If this threshold is low the likelihood of detection is great as only some of the values of a face are met (but it still may be a face). The problem here is that the number of false detections is likely to increase. A higher threshold will prefer more 'perfect' faces with more parameters met and will return more definite possibilities of true faces. The problem of this is that the variety of faces and poses do not adhere to the perfect face rules. A threshold value between these two extremities will be used most often. The algorithm for training the neural network follows:

> Image Scanning and Detection
> START
> - Input image for testing
> - Set Parameters for test
>> Set Threshold to determine how strict the detector is
>> Set number of pyramid levels
>> Set the start level (smaller number for smaller faces) of pyramid. Must not exceed Total number of levels.
>> Set pyramid resolution scale factor

- Build a resolution pyramid of the input image, each level of the pyramid decreasing the image resolution from Start level to No. of levels

- For each level of the pyramid
    Extract each rectangle from the image
    Normalise it
    Pass it to neural network
    If rectangle passed contains a face i.e. NET returns 0.9
    Scale rectangle to size appropriate for original image
    Add it to face bounding set

- Present result image with rectangles drawn on face bounding set.
- Any non-face detections forward to bootstrapping routine.
END

# 5    Face Detection System Implementation

Now that the details of a generic face detection system have been defined, we can proceed to outline the implementation of a novel prototype which implements much of the earlier theory and system components. The system has been programmed using MATLAB.

## 5.1    Data Preparation

The reason for this stage is to make the inputs to the system uniform in order for the network to obtain accurate results. This area will describe how datasets are gained to train the network and what way they are prepared for input to the system. This covers resizing, masking and normalising the face and non-face data. The accuracy of the detector relies heavily on this stage of the system. The quality of the training sets inputted into the network at this stage determines how well the detector will perform.

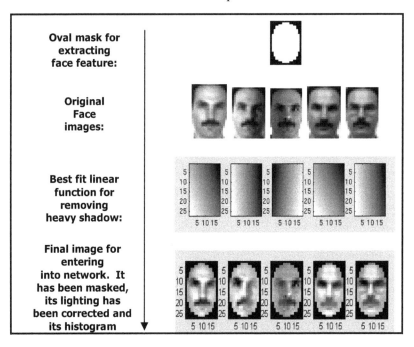

**Fig 5.1:** The steps of data preparation.

An ideal scenario would be to give the network as large a set of training examples as possible, in order to attain a comprehensive sampling of a larger representation of faces. To achieve this, images need to be resized and cut into 18x27 pixel sizes. 60 face images were used for entry at the data preparation stage. These are used to create 120 face training images by taking the left and right compliments of the original image. Each of these images has to be masked with a 18x27 pixel mask and normalised to give a clear face image. Figure 5.1 shows a representation of the data at each preparation level.

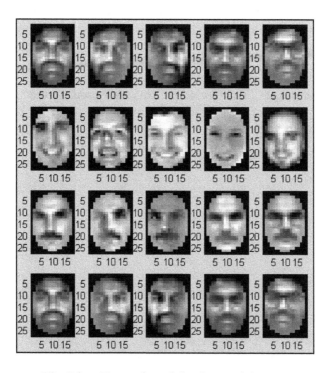

**Fig 5.2a:** Examples of the face training set

As can be seen, the best linear function is applied to each individual image and then subtracted out. This corrects some of the harsh lighting conditions and gives a clear representation of the image. The mask applied to each image clearly defines the face shape. The network will be looking for faces that fit this aspect. You can see the resultant images have approximately the same grey level distribution. The scanning part of the program employs these steps to each window that is scanned from every test image. The function is designed to equalise the intensity values across the window (see algorithm on normalisation earlier) and MATLAB code in Appendix A – normalise.m).

Pixels outside the oval mask are ignored so the values in this area are not considered when approximating the lighting correction. The linear function approximates the overall brightness of each part of the image being considered. The result is then subtracted from the window to compensate for the variety of lighting conditions. This normalisation technique is very important for the functioning of the network.

Fig 5.2a shows a few examples of the face training set after the data preparation stage. This technique was also used on the non-face examples to correct their lighting and also to mask them. They can be seen in Fig 5.2b.

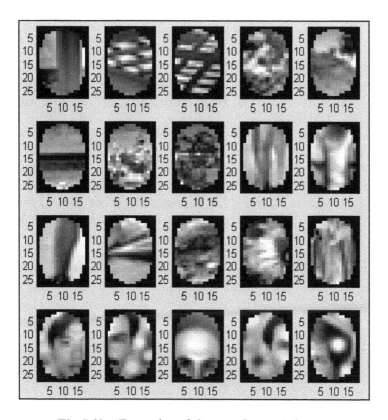

**Fig 5.2b:** Examples of the non-face training set

## 5.2 Bootstrapping Algorithm

Random non-face images (Fig 4.5) are used to train the early network. These were input intending the network to classify them as negative examples and to give an output of -0.9 (not face). However, the randomness of the structure of the images created did nothing to boost the accuracy of the network when early tests were run. The next step was to add a number of all black images to the training set. This approach proved more beneficial, and clearly provided a benefit to the network's ability to classify. The flat black image provided a baseline for the network to compare to when classifying. A more realistic set of training non-face images was subsequently found.

Fig 5.3 shows an early test result from the program. The image contains no faces just a typical background. If the program detected any positive results from this image they had to be non-faces.

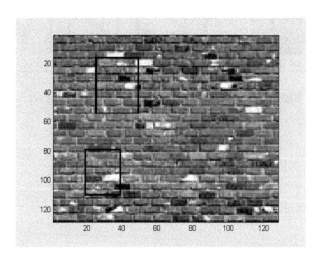

**Fig 5.3:** An early test result to find non-face examples

These detects are non-face examples with high information value that resemble the face vectors in the neural network. These 'valid' non-faces are more useful when presented as non-face training images. The non-face database can grow very large so this method guarantees that the non-face values are not redundant information for the network.

Fig 5.4 show an early test on an image with faces detected but there is also a high rate of detections of non-face images. This test was done early in the programs development so the size of the non-face database was small. This can explain the high miss rate. The image does however have a complex background, which illustrates what the system was up against.

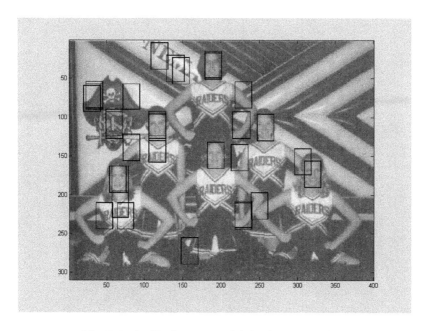

**Fig 5.4:** An Early test useful for bootstrapping

This method collects the mistakes the system is making. These new training examples improve the classifiers performance by steering it away from the mistakes it currently commits. The system learns not to classify these as faces in the future.

A set of 50 non-face images were flipped left to right and upside down to give a total number of 200 non-face images (see Appendix

A - facetrain.m and loadimages.m). Notice the range of images presented in Fig 5.2. You will notice pieces of scenery that are definitely not faces but you will also notice small partial images of faces. These images where gained using the bootstrapping algorithm in an attempt to reduce overlapping detections. They are after all not a complete face.

## 5.3   Training Algorithm

The classifiers task is to identify face test patterns from non-face test patterns based on vectors produced by training images. This training stage defines the network to carry out this task. At this stage we presume that our data set, both face and non-face, has been prepared and is ready for input to the network. The training program (see Appendix A – facetrain.m) loads all the required training data and starts to train the network.

As outlined before, a multi-layer perceptron network was used to perform the classification task. Each of the 400 input variables of each training image was entered in vector form. The network had 1 output unit and 25 hidden units. Each hidden and output unit computes a weighted sum of its input links and performs Tan sigmoidal thresholding on its output. The output unit returns a 0.9 if a face is detected and -0.9 if otherwise.

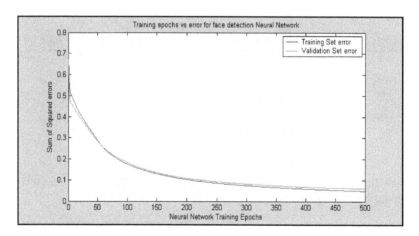

**Fig 5.5:** Network Result - Training error vs. epochs

The Network is trained with the back-propagation learning algorithm until the output error stabilises (or until training reaches 500 epochs). Fig 5.5 shows the training result. The sum of squared error rate on the training set over 500 epochs for the Validation set error (red) and Training Set error (blue). Note that around epoch 50 the validation set error surpasses the training set error. However the validation set error never increases from a previous time step and therefore the network proceeds to an approximate convergence. This suggests that the training set is good enough to detect a face image that is not contained in the training set by approximating the faces values to suit a positive detection.

After the training of the network, we can determine from the network parameters how well the training images were classified. The current performance of the network is shown in Table 5.1. Note that this is the most recent performance of the network with my final training set after extensive bootstrapping. The network performs much better at detecting non-faces. This is due to the amount of images made available in the dataset it is therefore more bias towards detecting non-faces. This should lead to a lower false positive rate than if the bias had been in the favour of face images instead.

|  | Number of Training images | Number successfully classified | Percentage of success |
|---|---|---|---|
| Face Detection Rate in Training | 120 | 112 | 93% |
| Non-face Detection Rate in Training | 200 | 193 | 96.5% |
| Overall Classification Rate | 320 | 305 | 95.3% |

**Table 5.1:** Training results

Now that the neural network has been trained, it can now be used to classify faces in test images.

## 5.4    Scanning and Detecting a face

Since the scanning window is fixed at 18x27 pixels, a means of scaling the image needed to be implemented so faces of multiple sizes can be detected in multiple sized images. This is implemented by scaling an image's resolution by a factor of 1.2. The image is scaled several times to realise detection of a 18x27 window at different image sizes. Fig 5.6 shows an image of 200x130 in pixel size. When it was passed through the scanning routine (*see appendix A – facescan.m*) its image pyramid for six levels is shown in Fig 5.7.

**Fig 5.6:** Original image

As you can see Level 1 is the original image with the same parameters and picture quality. But you will notice level 2 has parameters of 108 x 166 pixels. This is a result of the scale factor of 1.2. This scaling continues to level six where the resolution is approx 80x50. Keep in mind that the scanning routine will scan every 18x27 window at every level.

**Fig 5.7:** Resolution Pyramid

It's obvious that the classifier should not pick up an 18x27 face in level 1 as the face present is too large. The program should not classify any positive detects until the level has reached a certain point where the face's resolution lies in a 18x27 bounding box. In fact the test image was run through the program and returned one positive value at level 6. This result is shown below in Fig 5.8.

**Fig 5.8:** Successful detection at level 6 of pyramid

From the above result we can see that this technique is successful. Once the pyramid is created the image is scanned over and every rectangle of the image at each level is passed to be normalised, masked and passed to the neutral network for classification. The network then outputs a result of -0.9 to 0.9. This value is then thresholded by a threshold limit that determines the strictness of the program. If the value is positive the window detected as a face is bounded with a rectangle (shown above). This is shown on the original image not the level of the pyramid that it was detected.

This procedure is done multiple times on the image and therefore multiple detections are possible. This however means that the same face can and is detected more than once in different levels of the resolution pyramid or indeed the same level. The bounding co-ordinates are passed back to the calling procedure and stored. Once the scanning procedure has finished the original image is called and the bounding boxes are plotted over the image. The issue of lighting effects and how they would effect the result if the issue was not considered was addressed by creating a training set that had an abundance of data that needed their light corrected. Next, situations that required the need for the procedure to take place in the first place were tested (e.g. heavy lighting). Fig 5.9 to 5.11 show the images that were used to illustrate the problem of heavy lighting effects.

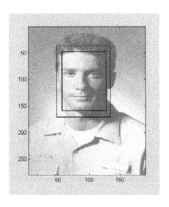 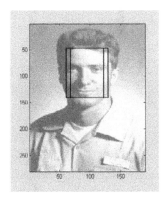

**Fig 5.9:** Image with Heavy light 1        **Fig 5.10:** Image with Heavy light 2

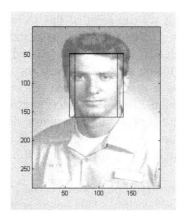

**Fig 5.1:** Image with No lighting effects

As you can see the program has successfully combated the problem of these lighting effects as the program has successfully detected the three examples.

# 5.5  Situations for testing

The program has been developed so that it can accept a colour or black and white jpeg image and return an image that show results in the form of the image with bounding boxes over detections and some parameters suggesting at what stage the detections where realised. Some factors governing the detection routine are now presented. These are:

## Number of Pyramid levels

This should be adjusted to suit the size of the image being tested. If the image is under, say, 300x300 pixels in size the number of levels can be set to about 6 as this will cover the sizes of faces in that image that can be classified as a face. If it is over this size, then it is better to set the pyramid higher to scale the bigger image to a point that a 18x27 can detect a face in a an image of that size. The option to set the start level of the pyramid here is available because in an image of 500x500 pixels the likelihood that a 18x27 face exists in that image is not good. In addition, the program takes longer to run in larger images if the start level is set as low. Redundant data is gained and useful processing time can be avoided this way.

## Scalefactor

The scalefactor can also be altered in the program. This was used in the initial testing stages to see what factor worked best. This defaults to 1.2.

## Threshold of classifier

This value of this parameter can be set can be set from 0.0 to 0.9. This determines if the value sent back from the classifier is enough to classify a tested window as a face. A low threshold will return more windows as a face and is more likely to pick up a detection of a face. A low threshold takes the output of the neural network and gives it a higher margin of error than a high threshold. It means that it is more likely to detect a face but it also more likely to return a false positive. It is more likely to classify a piece of scenery as a face. At a high threshold the program accuracy of real faces will be higher and false positives will be lower but it might not detect the face at all. Fig 5.12 shows the detector at a low threshold that will allow uncertain detects through.

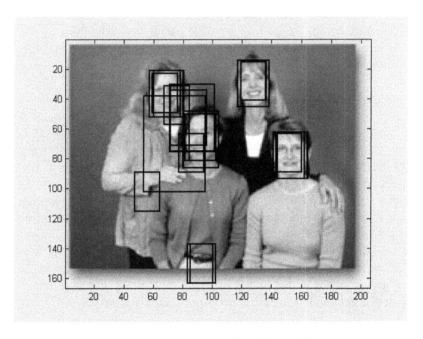

**Fig 5.12:** Detector at low threshold

You can see from the image that the faces that exist in the image are clearly defined and located by the detector but the amount of false positives in the image outweighs the amount of correct detects. Fig 5.13 shows the same image entered into the same network but the threshold at which detects are accepted has been increased.

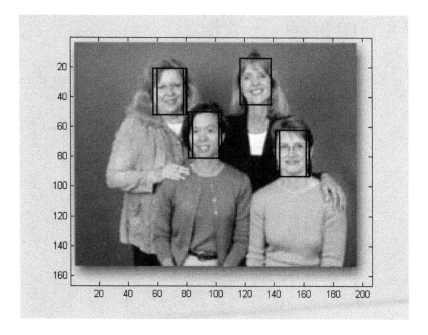

**Fig 5.13:** Image through higher threshold.

The image show that there is no false detects but there is overlapping of bounding boxes. This means the same face occupied a region that was scanned twice and both times the information of face data passed to the neural network was enough to warrant a successful detection.

## 5.6   Test Results

Fig 5.14 through to Fig 5.22 shows a range of example test results. Fig 5.14 is an image ideally suited to the face detection system, it has a simple background with nothing in it to confuse as a face and the face is facing forward (like most of the training set).

**Fig 5.14:** Image with simple background

Fig 5.15 however shows a face candidate amongst a complex background. It has the likelihood to return some false positives however with the training set available, the system was able to restrict it to a small number of false positives.

**Fig 5.15:** Image with Complex background

Fig 5.16 shows an image with more than one face – It needed to return multiple detects. Note the background of the image is not interfering with the image and will not give false positives.

**Fig 5.16:** Image with multiple detects

Fig 5.17 shows an image with a face which is undetected due to it position. If it had have been frontal it may have been detected.

**Fig 5.17:** No detect

Fig 5.18 shows that the detector could not classify a drawn face from a cartoon character. It also gave a few false positives.

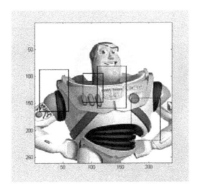

**Fig 5.18:** Test on Cartoon character

Fig 19 shows a successful detection of a smiling woman. This is an ideal type face for the system. No distractions exist.

**Fig 5.19:** Successful detection 1

Fig 5.19 – Fig 5.22 show some of the more successful detects that are ideally suited to the system. Fig 5.20 is a larger image than the rest with dimensions of 300x400 pixels. Here the total number of scale levels was set at 8 and it has detected the face really well (perhaps due to the simple background).

**Fig 5.20:** Successful detection 2

Fig 5.21 shows detection at different levels of the pyramid. It has detected them at different scales and positions. This shows that the network can generalise well.

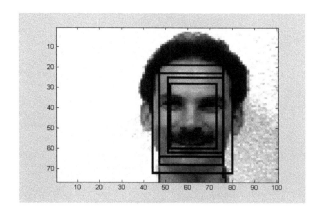

**Fig 5.21:** Successful detection 3.

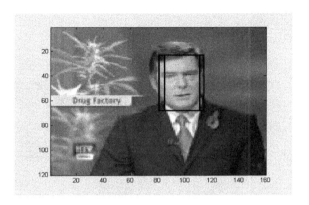

**Fig 5.22:** Successful detection 4

Fig 5.22 also shows detection at different levels of the pyramid clearly. It has detected them at different scales and positions thus demonstrating that the face detection system can generalise well.

## 5.7    Performance Results

The successfulness of any such detection system depends on how well the network is trained. The speed and accuracy of the system is dependant on a set of parameters that can be adjusted for different results. All training and detection routines were carried out on a PC with a 1.6Ghz Pentium 4 processor with 512 Mb of RAM. All the results where gained using the same Neural network so all the training datasets were the same. The threshold factor denotes how strict the network will be when it comes to classify the image. The testing highlighted which threshold values to use in making the system a more accurate robust face detector.

Table 5.2 shows the extent of the testing. Testing was performed on 100 images ranging from image containing a single face with simple backgrounds (see Fig 5.14) to images with complex backgrounds (Fig 5.15) images with multiple faces (Fig 5.16). Each Image had at least one face and these were between 150x150 and 400x400 pixels in size. A total pyramid level size of 6 was chosen with a start pyramid level of 1 and a scalefactor of 1.2 in all images. In total there were 230 faces to be detected.

| Threshold | Number of correct faces (from 230) | Rate | False positive per image (from 100) | Rate |
|-----------|------------------------------------|-------|-------------------------------------|-------|
| 0.0 | 220 | 0.956 | 84 | 0.84 |
| 0.1 | 209 | 0.909 | 75 | 0.75 |
| 0.2 | 196 | 0.852 | 63 | 0.63 |
| 0.3 | 181 | 0.787 | 41 | 0.41 |
| 0.4 | 179 | 0.778 | 29 | 0.29 |
| 0.5 | 154 | 0.670 | 15 | 0.15 |
| 0.6 | 102 | 0.443 | 12 | 0.12 |
| 0.7 | 56 | 0.243 | 4 | 0.04 |
| 0.8 | 32 | 0.139 | 0 | 0 |
| 0.9 | 9 | 0.039 | 0 | 0 |

**Table 5.2:** Testing results

From the results above it is clear that in order to achieve high detection rates in a range of images it also stands to detect more false positives. A very low threshold will detect the same amount of false detections as correct detections. At a high threshold the program gives less false positives but it will also probably fail to detect faces that were just below the threshold.

Achieving increased face detection rates comes at the cost of increased false positive rates. 220 of the 230 images where detected at 0.0 the lowest threshold. The resultant image from these detections contained a high rate of false detections. A high volume of overlapping bounding boxes showed a random and undefined set of detections. As the testing progressed up through the earlier thresholds (0.1-0.4) a definite pattern was suggested. For each step in the test the number of false positives greatly decreased but some detections were sacrificed. The faces that were sacrificed the most were usually smaller less defined face in group pictures.

At a very high threshold level, only nine faces were detected. Five of these where actually faces from the Yale face database and therefore a part of the training set. This proves that through an even bigger dataset of faces the program can become even more accurate. It was found that a threshold of between 0.5-0.6 gives the best range of results out of the threshold set tested. They give a more obvious set of results and continue to detect large faces that produce good data vectors. Detects that are found within this threshold reflect data that is in the training set.

# 6   Conclusion

The algorithm presented in this book can detect between 67% and 85% of faces from images of varying size, background and quality with an acceptable number of false detections. It can detect between 'face' and 'non-face'. One of the most important components of the system is the normalisation routine. This is a technique that makes training data and test data uniform and where lighting is involved it can drastically affect the classifying of images. The neural network approach is known to be highly sensitive to the grey levels in an image however by subjecting each trained and tested image to the routine introduced here - the system sidestepped the problem.

The Yale Face database is an excellent resource for the range of faces, poses and lighting effects on the images. The bootstrapping method used to gain non-face datasets proved very successful as early results were very poor until use was made of the new training data. The speed of the system was quite good when average sized images and searched through a limited amount of levels. Testing larger images involves merely changed a few parameters to miss the first few levels of a larger image. This can become as fast as an average sized image and produce some good quality attempts at classification.

A drawback of a non-commercial prototype such as introduced here is the number of false positives. It was found that images with complex backgrounds produced a lot of false detects. Even when these images were added these to the non-face dataset, similar detections in another image occurred. Perhaps a larger data set of face and non-face images would correct this. The dataset could be a wider range of poses with not just near frontal views. The current program can incorporate new images such as these without major modification. Further research into face anatomy and how humans perceive a human face to be, could help explore the hidden units in the Neural Network further. Tests on the pixel areas that each hidden unit explores to match face images is a research area ripe for further investigation.

# References

[1] T. Sakai, M. Nagao, and T. Kanade, Computer analysis and classification of photographs of human faces 1972

[2] Md. Al-Amin BHUIYAN, Shin-yo MUTO , Haruki UENO. *Face Detection and Facial Feature Localisation for Human-machine Interface.* National Institute of Informatics

[3] Erik Hjelmas, Boon Kee Low. *Face Detection: A Survey* Department of Informatics, University of Oslo, Norway. April 2001

[4] Harley R.Miller, Arthur R.Weeks. *The Pocket Handbook of Image processing Algorithms.* ISBN 0-13-6422403

[5] Kah-kay Sung and Tomaso Poggio , Example –based Learning for View-based Human face Detection. Dec 1994

[6] Y. Wang and B. Yuan. *Fast Method for face location and tracking by distributed Behaviour-based agents.* IEE Proceedings vision, Image and Signal Processing. April 1995.

[7] Craw, H. Ellis, and J. R. Lishman, Automatic extraction of face-feature, *Pattern Recog. Lett.* Feb. 1987

[8] Leung, T.K, Burl, M.C and P.Perona. *Finding Faces in Cluttered Scenes Using Random Labeled Graph Matching.* Fifth Intl. Conf. on Computer Vision, Cambridge, MA. 1995

[9] C. H. Lee, J. S. Kim, and K. H. Park, Automatic human face location in a complex background, Pattern Recog. 29, 1996,

[10] X. Jiang, M. Binkert, B. Achermann, and H. Bunke, Towards detection of glasses in facial images, Pattern Anal. Appl., 2000

[11] Z. Jing and R. Mariani, *Glasses detection and extraction by deformable contour,* in Proceedings of the 15th International Conference on Pattern Recognition, 2000.

[12] E. Hjelmas and J. Wroldsen, Recognizing faces from the eyes only, in Proceedings of the 11th Scandinavian Conference on Image Analysis, 1999.

[13] Lanitis, C. J. Taylor, T. F. Cootes, Automatic tracking, coding and reconstruction of human faces, using flexible appearance models, IEEE Electron. Lett. 1994,

[14] Yale face database,
http://cvc.yale.edu/projects/yalefaces/yalefaces.html

[15] Asim Shankar, Priyendra Singh Deshwal. Face Detection in images : Neural networks & Support Vector Machines April 2002

[16] L. Sirovich and M. Kirby, Low-dimensional procedure for the characterization of human faces, 1987, 519–524.

[17] H. Martin Hunke *Locating and Tracking of Human Faces with Neural Networks.* 1994

[18] H. A. Rowley, S. Baluja, and T. Kanade, *Neural network-based face detection, IEEE Trans. Pattern* January 1998,

[19] L. C. De Silva, K. Aizawa, and M. Hatori, Detection and tracking of facial features by using a facial feature model and deformable circular template, IEICE Trans. Inform. Systems E78–D(9), 1995, 1195–1207.

[20] M. Kass, A. Witkin, and D. Terzopoulos, Snakes: active contour models, in Proc. of 1st Int Conf. on Computer Vision, London, 1987.

[21] T. F. Cootes and C. J. Taylor, Active shape models—'smart snakes,' in Proc. of British Machine Vision Conference, 1992, pp. 266–275.

[22] L. Sirovich and M. Kirby, Low-dimensional procedure for the characterization of human faces, J. Opt. Soc. Amer. 4, 1987, 519–524.

[23] R. Feraud, O. Bernier, and D. Collobert, A constrained generative model applied to face detection, Neural Process. Lett. 5, 1997, 73–81.

[24] D. Roth, M.-H. Yang, and N. Ahuja, A SNoW-based face detector, in Advances in Neural Information Processing Systems 12 (NIPS 12), MIT Press, Cambridge, MA, 2000.

[25] N. Duta and A. K. Jain, Learning the human face concept from black and white images, in Proc. of International Conference on Pattern Recognition, 1998.

[26] E. Osuna, R. Freund, and F. Girosi, Training support vector machines: An application to face detection, in IEEE Proc. of Int. Conf. on Computer Vision and Pattern Recognition, 6, 1997.

[27] V. Vapnik, The Nature of Statistical Learning Theory. Springer-Verlag, New York, 1995.

[28] G. Burel and D. Carel, Detection and localization of faces on digital images, Pattern Recog. Lett. 15, 1994, 963–967.

# Appendix A - MATLAB Code for Neural Network Based Face Detector.

1. Facetrain.m
2. Trainnn.m
3. Facesan.m
4. Creatnn.m
5. Buildmask.m
6. Classifynn.m
7. Normalize.m
8. Loadimages.m
9. Showimages.m
10. Augmentlr.m
11. Augmentud.m

%

---

% facetrain.m
%

---

% Desc:    This the main training for the network for the face detector. It
% loads all required training files , builds the data structures.  It then
% trains and tests the neural Network
%

%

---

%                              Setup
%

---

% Neural net constants
% These are used to test tresholds for faces (FACE_T) and non face(FACE_F)
FACE_T =  0.9;
FACE_F = -0.9;


% Load the image oval mask
MASK = buildmask;          % Builds a 18x27 oval image mask
NI   = size(find(MASK),1);    % Determines the size of oval in the mask

% _____

%                      Image Loading
% _____

% Load the face images from file. The method below to ensure
% efficient input was used.  It is passed to the function load images
%where it decifers the format

FACES = loadimages('./scaled/s', {'01' '02' '04' '07' '11' '99'}, ...

{'c' 'l' 'r' 'n' 'g' 'i' 'j' 'k' 'l' 'm' 'n'}, 'PNG', 1);

% This function flips image L -> R to give another version of it to expand the
% data set. see augmentlr
FACES = augmentlr(FACES);

% Normalize the faces
[NORM_FACES, SHADING] = normalize(FACES, MASK);

% This Builds an image vector from the rectanglar image array. It is used
% to return yasble data to train the nueral net
FACEV = buildimvector(NORM_FACES, MASK);

% This builds a result vector to match the image vector
FACER = buildresvector(NORM_FACES, FACE_T);

% Load the non-face images, normalize, and set training vectors

NFACES = loadimages('./scaled/n', ...
        {'01' '02' '03' '04' '05' '06' '07' '08' '09' '10' '11' '12' '13' '14' ...
        '15' '16' '17' '18' '19' '20' '21' '22' '23' '24' '25' '26' '27' '28' ...
        '29' '30' '31' '32' '33' '34' '35' '36' '37' '38' '39' '40'}, ...
        {'x'} {'y'}, 'PNG', 1);

% This function flips image L -> R to give another version of it to expand the
% data set. see augmentlr
NFACES = augmentlr(NFACES);

% This function flips image upside-down to give another version of it to expand the
% data set. see augmentud
NFACES = augmentud(NFACES);

% Normalize
[NORM_NFACES, NSHADING] = normalize(NFACES, MASK);

% This Builds an image vector from the rectanglar image array.  It is used
% to return yasble data to train the nueral net
NFACEV = buildimvector(NORM_NFACES, MASK);

% This builds a result vector to match the image vector
NFACER = buildresvector(NORM_NFACES, FACE_F);

% Display images used as training
 showimages(NORM_FACES,  5, 10, 1, 50, 1);
 showimages(NORM_NFACES, 5, 5, 1, 25, 2);
% pause;

%

_____

%                     Neural Net Training
% _____
% Build a neural net and train it
% This neural net gets passed pixels for face (NI) approx 400, 25 hidden
% layers, 1 output layer and thresholds for face and non face (defined as
% constants above)
NET = createnn(NI, 25, 1, FACE_F, FACE_T);

% trains until 500 epochs or or there is a decrease in performance on the
% validation set
[NET,PERF, ERR] = trainnn(NET,[NFACEV FACEV], [NFACER FACER], .10, 500);

% Plots the performace data for the training of the network
figure(3); plot(PERF(:,1),PERF(:,2),'b-',PERF(:,1),PERF(:,3),'r-');
figure(4); plot(ERR (:,1),ERR (:,2),'b-',ERR (:,1),ERR (:,3),'r-');

% _____

%                     Performance Testing

```
%  _____

% Test performance - for now just test on original images; extend to
% an image pyramid and return upper left corner of all 27x18 face
% bounding boxes.  It tests the training data (face and non-face) and
% determines positive or negative detection rate.

NUM_FACES  = size(FACES,2);
NUM_NFACES = size(NFACES,2);

t0 = clock; ferr = 0;
for i=1:NUM_FACES,                      % test faces
  TEST = classifynn(NET, FACES{i}, MASK,1,1);
  fprintf(1, '(Target, Test, Match): (%f,%f,%d)\n', FACE_T, TEST,
TEST > 0);
  ferr = ferr + (TEST < 0);
end

nferr = 0;
for i=1:NUM_NFACES,                          % test non-faces
  TEST = classifynn(NET, NFACES{i}, MASK,1,1);
  fprintf(1, '(Target, Test, Match): (%f,%f,%d)\n', FACE_F, TEST,
TEST < 0);
  nferr = nferr + (TEST > 0);
end


% Performace charts are detailed below it show how well the
training data
% is classified (more non-face images so it is bias towards non-face)

fprintf(1,    '\n(Face    Err,    Nonface    Err,    Total    Err):
(%1.3f,%1.3f,%1.3f)\n', ...
          ferr./NUM_FACES,    nferr./NUM_NFACES,    (ferr   +
nferr)./(NUM_FACES + NUM_NFACES));
fprintf(1,    'Time    to    classify    %d    images:    %5.3f\n',
NUM_FACES+NUM_NFACES, etime(clock,t0));
```

```
% trainnn.m
% Desc:  Trains a neural net given a training set with target values
%        and randomly selects training and validation data, training
%               either for the max number of networks, network
convergence,
%               or increase in validation error.  Returns network and
performance.
%
%               [NET,PERF,            ERR]         =
trainnn(NET,IMVECTOR,TVECTOR,percent_val,iter)
function        [NET,PERF,            ERR]         =
trainnn(NET,IMVECTOR,TVECTOR,percent_val,iter)

% Setup validation and test sets
N_IMS = size(IMVECTOR,2);
CHOICE  = rand(1,N_IMS) > percent_val;
V_TRAIN = find(CHOICE);
V_VALID = find(1-CHOICE);
IM_TRAIN_V = IMVECTOR(:,V_TRAIN);
IM_TRAIN_R = TVECTOR (:,V_TRAIN);
IM_VALID_V = IMVECTOR(:,V_VALID);
IM_VALID_R = TVECTOR (:,V_VALID);
fprintf(1,'Training set quantity:  #%d\n', size(IM_TRAIN_V,2));
fprintf(1,'Validation set quantity: #%d\n', size(IM_VALID_V,2));

% Setup net parameters
NET.trainParam.epochs = 1;
NET.trainParam.goal   = 0.0001;
TRAIN_OUT = simnn(NET,IM_TRAIN_V);
VALID_OUT = simnn(NET,IM_VALID_V);
PERF = [];
ERR  = [];
PERF    =    [PERF;    0,    (1-(sum(abs(TRAIN_OUT-
IM_TRAIN_R)./1.8)./(size(TRAIN_OUT,2)))), ...
         (1-(sum(abs(VALID_OUT-
IM_VALID_R)./1.8)./(size(VALID_OUT,2))))];
ERR     =    [ERR;    0,    ((sum(abs(TRAIN_OUT-
IM_TRAIN_R))./(size(TRAIN_OUT,2))).^2), ...
```

```
      ((sum(abs(VALID_OUT-
IM_VALID_R))./(size(VALID_OUT,2))).^2)];

% Train for specified number of iterations
for i=1:iter,
  fprintf(1,'Starting iteration %d\n', i);
  drawnow;
  [NET, TR] = train(NET, IM_TRAIN_V, IM_TRAIN_R);
  TRAIN_OUT = simnn(NET,IM_TRAIN_V);
  VALID_OUT = simnn(NET,IM_VALID_V);
  %[TRAIN_OUT; IM_TRAIN_R]
  %[VALID_OUT; IM_VALID_R]
  PERF    =    [PERF;    i,    (1-(sum(abs(TRAIN_OUT-
IM_TRAIN_R)./1.8)./(size(TRAIN_OUT,2))))), ...
          (1-(sum(abs(VALID_OUT-
IM_VALID_R)./1.8)./(size(VALID_OUT,2))))];
  ERR     =    [ERR;     i,    ((sum(abs(TRAIN_OUT-
IM_TRAIN_R))./(size(TRAIN_OUT,2))).^2), ...
          ((sum(abs(VALID_OUT-
IM_VALID_R))./(size(VALID_OUT,2))).^2)];
end
```

```
%  _____
% Facescan.m
%  _____
% Desc:   Build an image resolution pyramid and scan the pyramid
for
%         faces given the neural net, image, mask, and threshold -
1<THR<1
%
% [RECT, IMR] = facescan(NET, IM, MASK, THR, LEVELS,
START, SCALEFACT, STEP)

function [RECT, IMR] = facescan(NET, IM, MASK, THR,
LEVELS, START, SCALEFACT, STEP)

% START can start at 1 but this is only for small faces in the image
(note
% must not exceed tot number of levels)
% THR determines how strict the detector (say low 0.4 - high 0.9)
% STEP works along with scalfactor best at 2
% SCALEFACT determines how much the resolution is scaled in
each level of
% pyramid good at 1.1 or 1.2
% LEVELS determines how


START = 3;
THR = 0.6;
STEP = 2;
SCALEFACT = 1.2;

LEVELS = 4;
load MASK;
load NET;

%imagename = input('Enter the image name : ','s');
%colourimage =(imread('./scaled/',{imagename},'JPG'));


colourimage =(imread('./scaled/test.JPG'));
```

```
bw1 = rgb2gray(colourimage);
testimage = double(bw1);

%testimage = double(imread('./scaled/col1.JPG'));
IM = testimage;

% Setup
PYR_MAX = LEVELS; % A good choice is 6
MROWS = size(MASK,1);
MCOLS = size(MASK,2);
IROWS = size(IM, 1);
ICOLS = size(IM, 2);
RECT = [];

% Build the image pyramid
SCALE = SCALEFACT; % A good choice is 1.2
PYR{1} = IM;
XRANGE{1} = 1:1:ICOLS;
YRANGE{1} = 1:1:IROWS;
[MX{1},MY{1}] = meshgrid(XRANGE{1}, YRANGE{1});
for i=2:PYR_MAX,
        XRANGE{i} = 1:SCALE.^(i-1):ICOLS;
        YRANGE{i} = 1:SCALE.^(i-1):IROWS;
        [MX{i},MY{i}] = meshgrid(XRANGE{i}, YRANGE{i});
        PYR{i}  =  interp2(MX{1},  MY{1},  PYR{1},  MX{i},
MY{i});
end

% View pyramid
%figure(1);
%colormap(gray);
%showimages(PYR, 2, 3, 1, 6, 1);
%drawnow;
%pause;

% Scan the pyramid
for im_num = START:PYR_MAX,
  fprintf(1, '\n\nImage: %d\n', im_num);
  for im_row = 1:STEP:size(PYR{im_num},1)-MROWS+1,
```

71

```
    fprintf(1, ' R:%d', im_row);
    for im_col = 1:STEP:size(PYR{im_num},2)-MCOLS+1,
        TEST = classifynn(NET, PYR{im_num}, MASK, im_row,
im_col);
        if (TEST > THR)
            fprintf(1, '\n    -(INUM,R,C,TEST):  [%d]  (%d,%d)  =>
%5.3f ',im_num, im_row, im_col, TEST);
            RECT                =                [RECT;
(im_row/size(YRANGE{im_num},2))*size(YRANGE{1},2), ...

(im_col/size(XRANGE{im_num},2))*size(XRANGE{1},2), ...
            ((im_row+MROWS-
1)/size(YRANGE{im_num},2))*size(YRANGE{1},2), ...
            ((im_col+MCOLS-
1)/size(XRANGE{im_num},2))*size(XRANGE{1},2), ...
            TEST];
        end
    end
  end
end

% Plot the bounding boxes in an image to return
IMR = IM;
for i=1:size(RECT,1),
  SR = ceil(RECT(i,1));
  ER = ceil(RECT(i,3));
  SC = ceil(RECT(i,2));
  EC = ceil(RECT(i,4));
  IMR(SR,SC:EC) = 0;
  IMR(ER,SC:EC) = 0;
  IMR(SR:ER,SC) = 0;
  IMR(SR:ER,EC) = 0;
end

% Plot the image
figure(2);
colormap(gray);
imagesc(IMR);
drawnow;
```

```
% creatnn.m
% Desc:   Creates a neural net with the given parameters
%
% NET = createnn(input, hidden, output, min, max)
function NET = createnn(input, hidden, output, min, max)

PR = repmat([min,max],input,1);
S = [hidden output];
T = {'tansig' 'tansig'};
NET = newff(PR,S,T,'traingdm');
```

```matlab
% buildmask.m
% Desc:   Builds an oval mask for face images
%
% MASK = buildmask()
function MASK = buildmask()

% An 18x27 mask
MASK = ...
    [0 0 0 0 0 0 0 0 0 0 0 0 0 0 0 0 0 0; ...
     0 0 0 0 0 0 1 1 1 0 0 0 0 0 0 0; ...
     0 0 0 0 0 1 1 1 1 1 1 0 0 0 0 0; ...
     0 0 0 1 1 1 1 1 1 1 1 1 1 0 0 0; ...
     0 0 0 1 1 1 1 1 1 1 1 1 1 0 0 0; ...
     0 0 1 1 1 1 1 1 1 1 1 1 1 1 0 0; ...
     0 0 1 1 1 1 1 1 1 1 1 1 1 1 0 0; ...
     0 0 1 1 1 1 1 1 1 1 1 1 1 1 0 0; ...
     0 1 1 1 1 1 1 1 1 1 1 1 1 1 1 0; ...
     0 1 1 1 1 1 1 1 1 1 1 1 1 1 1 0; ...
     0 1 1 1 1 1 1 1 1 1 1 1 1 1 1 0; ...
     0 1 1 1 1 1 1 1 1 1 1 1 1 1 1 0; ...
     0 1 1 1 1 1 1 1 1 1 1 1 1 1 1 0; ...
     0 1 1 1 1 1 1 1 1 1 1 1 1 1 1 0; ...
     0 1 1 1 1 1 1 1 1 1 1 1 1 1 1 0; ...
     0 1 1 1 1 1 1 1 1 1 1 1 1 1 1 0; ...
     0 1 1 1 1 1 1 1 1 1 1 1 1 1 1 0; ...
     0 1 1 1 1 1 1 1 1 1 1 1 1 1 1 0; ...
     0 1 1 1 1 1 1 1 1 1 1 1 1 1 1 0; ...
     0 0 1 1 1 1 1 1 1 1 1 1 1 1 0 0; ...
     0 0 1 1 1 1 1 1 1 1 1 1 1 1 0 0; ...
     0 0 1 1 1 1 1 1 1 1 1 1 1 1 0 0; ...
     0 0 0 1 1 1 1 1 1 1 1 1 1 0 0 0; ...
     0 0 0 1 1 1 1 1 1 1 1 1 1 0 0 0; ...
     0 0 0 0 0 1 1 1 1 1 1 0 0 0 0 0; ...
     0 0 0 0 0 0 1 1 1 0 0 0 0 0 0 0; ...
     0 0 0 0 0 0 0 0 0 0 0 0 0 0 0 0      ];


% classifynn.m
% Desc:   From a given image, returns the classification value
```

```
%
% TEST = classifynn(NET, IM, MASK)
function TEST = classifynn(NET, IM, MASK, srow, scol)

% First normalize the face

V{1} = IM(srow:srow+26,scol:scol+17);
[V, PLANE] = normalize(V, MASK);

% Now test it
TEST = simnn(NET, V{1}(find(MASK)));
```

```
% normalise.m
% Desc:    Normalises an image by removing shading plane and
adjusting
%       histogram to scale to min/max [0,1]
%
% [OUT] = normalize(IN, MASK)
function [OUT, SHADING] = normalize(IN, MASK)

% Retrieve the indices for the given mask
IND = find(MASK);

% Set up matrices for planar projection calculation
% i.e. Ax = B  so  x = (A'*A)^-1 * A'*B
x = 1:1:size(IN{1},2);
y = 1:1:size(IN{1},1);
[mx,my] = meshgrid(x,y);
mxc = mx(IND);
myc = my(IND);
mcc = ones(size(myc));
A = [mxc, myc, mcc];

% Cycle through each image removing shading plane
% and adjusting histogram
for i=1:size(IN,2),

    % Calculate plane: z = ax + by + c
    B = IN{i}(IND);
    x = inv(A'*A)*A'*B;
    a = x(1); b = x(2); c = x(3);

    %This is the color plane itself
    SHADING{i} = mx.*a + my.*b + c;

    %This is the image minus the color plane
    %(the constant will be normalized out in histogram recentering)
    OUT{i} = IN{i} - (mx.*a + my.*b + c);

    % Now, recenter the histogram
    maximum = max(max(OUT{i}.*MASK));
```

```
    minimum  =  min(min(OUT{i}.*MASK));        %minimum  =
min(min(OUT{i}))
    diff = maximum - minimum;
    OUT{i} = ((OUT{i}-minimum)./diff).*MASK;

end
```

```
% loadimages.m
% Desc:   Loads a set of images into an array given
%         a prefix, suffix, and highest index filename.
%
% IM = loadimages(prefix, subject, letter, suffix, show)
function IM = loadimages(prefix, subject, letter, suffix, show)

clear IM;

% Load the image set
for i = 1:size(subject,2),
   for j = 1:size(letter,2),
     IM{(i-1)*size(letter,2)+j} = double(imread([prefix, subject{i}, '-
', letter{j}, '.', suffix]));
   end
end
```

```
% showimages.m
% Desc:   Displays an image array
%

% showimages(IM, xdim, ydim, start, end, fign)
function showimages(IM, xdim, ydim, start, endn, fign)

% Show the image set if fign is valid
if (fign>0)
  figure(fign);
  for i=start: endn,
    subplot(xdim,ydim,i-start+1);
    imagesc(IM{i});
    colormap gray;
  end
end
```

```
% augmentlr.m
% Desc:    Augments an image array with the L<->R reversed
images
%

% IM_NEW = augmentlr(IM)
function IM = augmentlr(IM)

num = size(IM,2);
nrows = size(IM{1},1);
ncols = size(IM{1},2);

for i=1:num,
        IM{i+num} = IM{i}(1:1:nrows,ncols:-1:1);
end
```

```
% agumentud.m
% Desc:   Augments an image array with the upside down reversed
images
%
% IM_NEW = augment(IM)
function IM = augmentud(IM)

num = size(IM,2);
nrows = size(IM{1},1);
ncols = size(IM{1},2);

for i=1:num,
        IM{i+num} = IM{i}(nrows:-1:1,1:1:ncols);
end
```